A
PAST
WORTH
TELLING

Mary Ann Niemczura, Ph.D.

abbott press®

A DIVISION OF WRITER'S DIGEST

Abbott Press books may be ordered through booksellers or by contacting:

Abbott Press
1663 Liberty Drive
Bloomington, IN 47403
www.abbottpress.com
Phone: 1-866-697-5310

Because of the dynamic nature of the Internet, any web addresses or links contained in this book may have changed since publication and may no longer be valid. The views expressed in this work are solely those of the author and do not necessarily reflect the views of the publisher, and the publisher hereby disclaims any responsibility for them.

Any people depicted in stock imagery provided by Thinkstock are models, and such images are being used for illustrative purposes only.
Certain stock imagery © Thinkstock.

ISBN: 978-1-4582-1299-3 (sc)
ISBN: 978-1-4582-1298-6 (hc)
ISBN: 978-1-4582-1297-9 (e)

Library of Congress Control Number: 2013921593

Printed in the United States of America.

Abbott Press rev. date: 2/21/2014

CONTENTS

DEDICATION

I dedicate this to my husband, Russell, whose love, patience, and advice were most valued in the writing process. You are a pearl of great value as my mother once remarked. Your cover photo of Beaver Lake Nature Center evokes fond memories.

To my children Tom and Emily who offered inspiration and gave encouragement along the way. I love you dearly, my honey cake and sugar plum. Thank you for cheering me on.

To my sisters who read some of the poems and gave me ideas for others. Sheila and Jean, you are the best. We had good times together.

To all my family, friends and colleagues along life's journey who read the poems and offered positive feedback, especially Jerry. Thanks for supporting my efforts.

EPIGRAPH

Give the world the best you have, and it may never be enough;
Give the world the best you've got anyway.

(from Mother Teresa's *Anyway* Poem)

FOREWORD

Today, more than ever, there is a greater understanding of the importance of the family and its relevance in helping children to become mature and strong contributing adults to our society. Though this awareness has only received greater attention from health care professionals and the media in recent years, it was a common tenet among families in past generations.

Through a collection of personal poems that span four family generations in the Northeast, Colorado, and Europe, the author shares with us those experiences, both as a youngster and as an adult, that helped shape her as a person and influenced her strong convictions of fairness, commitment, and individual accountability. The importance of family is evident in the author's poems at all stages in both her personal life and professional career.

Her writing is joyful and uplifting, but poignant at times. To her credit, she covers life's winding road with humor and reality.

Hopefully, Mary Ann Niemczura's delightful collection will "evoke fond memories" of our own youth and even serve in some instances as a guide for dealing with similar challenges.

Jerome F. Melvin, Ph.D.
Retired Superintendent of Schools
North Syracuse Central School District
North Syracuse, N.Y.

Poetry is meant to make a person stop and reflect. The poet stops to conjure up a vision of some event. The listener stops to hear the poem, then to hold it and tie it to memory. All are now bonded with a new view of life, saying "now there is a poem. I own it. Me."

The extended Niemczura family are the heirs to the great migration from Poland in the twentieth century, which largely erased the personal connection to our collective past. Let's create a new bridge between generations by collecting these memories and sharing them. We all own this history.

Joe Niemczura, RN, MS
Instructor, School of Nursing, University of Hawaii at Manoa
Author of *The Hospital at the End of the World*

INTRODUCTION

Childhood in rural Western Massachusetts in the 1940s and early 1950s offered carefree days filled with playing, learning and exploring with minimal adult supervision. Today children seldom experience such freedom and have so many more structured group activities and adults to run their lives. With advancements in technology, today's young people engage in activities that I never envisioned when growing up. There are advantages to being allowed to play outside on our own as we did in Sturbridge, Monson and Palmer in Massachusetts. We learned to problem solve and settle disputes when they arose. We had an appreciation for nature and nature's creatures. We savored horehound drops, penny candy, Mary Ann Cookies, crackers and pickles from the barrel at the Old Sturbridge Village General Store with the wooden Indian Chief outside.

This poetical memoir recalls fond childhood memories in Massachusetts as seen through my eyes and those of my sisters. These are followed by life in Colorado, Germany and Central New York. It is intended to document those memories for future generations and for anyone interested in such tales. The result may evoke fond memories of one's own youth.

As a teacher of German for forty-seven years, I included a few poems of memorable teaching experiences both in the U.S. and in Germany as a Fulbright teacher. Our two children became fluent German speakers after living in Germany for two years and attending German schools. They became world travelers and tolerant individuals in the process.

MASSACHUSETTS
MEMORIES

My parents met and married in Boston where my father had just graduated Boston University and my mother had finished nursing school and began working as a Registered Nurse. When they first met at a university dance, my father knew my mother was from Monson and that was not too far from Palmer. He decided to ask our mother out on a date but looked up the wrong name in the phone book. I asked him what he did. He told me he took out Marie the first night and the second night he phoned and dated our mother. We're happy he married the right one.

It was complicated

They met in Boston
And quickly filled
Their dance cards
For the evening.

Discovered they lived
In nearby towns.
Forgot her phone number
Looked her up in the

Phone book. Problem.
Was she Marie or Mary?
Went out with Marie
Even though she was

A stranger to him.
Phoned Mary next,
The right one.
Later married her.

Money was scarce after the Depression and college years so our parents married the same afternoon our father graduated college. She wore a navy blue suit, white silk blouse, gardenia corsage and her strawberry blond hair high in curls on the top of her head. She was beautiful; he was handsome.

A Gardenia Corsage

Young and in love
The Depression
Came. Money was scarce.
She was a registered nurse

And he graduated college.
Met and married in Boston
She wore a navy blue
Suit, white silk blouse

With a gardenia corsage.
Their marriage spanned
Almost five decades.
My father's joke was

He married my mother
For her money. Two
Hundred dollars was a
Big sum in those days.

The clothesline behind our Sturbridge house held the laundry smelling of fresh air. At the end of the day, our mother put it all in the straw laundry basket to empty and fold in the darkened living room as we watched the small black and white television. One evening, a scream came out of her throat and laundry went up in the air. We all screamed at the snake in the house.

Laundry Basket

Big straw laundry basket
Under the clothesline
Outdoors in the sun.
Fresh outdoor smell.

Mom took the
Laundry down
Just after supper
Unaware of the visitor.

While viewing
Black and white,
A sudden commotion
Ensued with

Laundry flying
Everywhere.
Mom shrieking
SNAKE.

Dad to the rescue
With ax in hand,
Moved two pieces
Outside.

We loved bundling into snowsuits, mittens and hats to play outside in the Massachusetts winter. We filled our yard one day with snowmen of all sizes and then counted them.

Twenty-five Snowmen

Bundled in snowsuits
Sliding down hills
On our wooden sleds
Rosy red cheeks

And cold hands
Through the mittens
Which were wet
From building

Twenty-five
Snowmen and
Summoned inside,
We warmed ourselves

In front of the
Fireplace.
Played outside
All day long.

In snowy
Sturbridge.
Those were
The days.

One summer weekend morning when our parents were still in bed, we went outside to play and decided to bring them a present of the orange lizards which crawled everywhere in the woods behind the house. Our gift in a jar of about forty-five of these tiny creatures was not exactly appreciated. We were told to bring them back outside.

Surprise Gift

Playing outdoors
In the woods
In Sturbridge
Was great fun.

Decided to give
Our parents
A surprise gift
One morning.

Arose early to
Search the
Woods for the
Orange-colored

Salamanders.
Brought them back
Forty-five squirming
In a jar.

Woke them up to
Show them the creatures.
Outside
With them they said.

We loved to go blueberry picking with our parents. Each of us had a tiny metal pail to their huge ones. We were to fill them up. By the end of the day, our pails were fairly empty but our tummies were full and our mouths were blue.

Little Blue Mouths

Each had a tiny
Metal pail for
The blueberries.
We picked.

Our parents
Kept watchful
Glances as
They filled

Large pails
Of juicy blueberries
For pies.
Pails mainly

Empty, we
Smiled at them
With blue mouths
And fingers.

When I first saw the red berries, I brought a few to my mother for identification. She said it was safe to consume them. So we did. They had a decidedly mint flavor.

Pretty Red

Their red color
Caught my attention
Out in the woods
Behind our house.

Red checkerberries
With white flesh
And minty taste.
Found them on

The ground under
The fallen leaves
And collected a
Few of these

Tasty treasures.
Rural Massachusetts
Revealed so many
Surprises.

I wanted to win at the card game called Authors but was not always successful in doing so. This time I decided I would win by sitting on one of the cards. After the cheating was discovered, I was sent to my room while my sisters were allowed to play. Life was not always fair.

Sitting on the Card

Near the built-in
Red desk in
The kitchen
We sat

Playing Authors
Card game.
Alcott, Hawthorne,
Irving, Cooper and others.

We learned their
Names. I liked to
Win and made
Certain I did

By sitting on one card.
My sisters protested.
My mother scolded. I
Had to leave the game.

At the end of Cedar Street where we lived in Sturbridge was the Old Sturbridge Village. Homes from an earlier era and costumes on the people, it was always intriguing to take a school field trip there. We all wanted one of the horseshoe nail rings the blacksmith forged each of us. There was no entry fee in those early days.

The Blacksmith

Our third grade class
Walked one mile on a
Field trip to the
Old Sturbridge Village.

We marveled at the
Costumes of bygone
Eras. The general
Store with the

Wooden Indian standing
Guard, pickles in barrels,
Penny candy, horehound
Drops. But the best

Was watching the village
Blacksmith make
Horseshoe nail rings
For each of us.

In Massachusetts, we learned to write cursive in first grade with big yellow pencils in our hands. Printing was not taught. But we had penmanship classes and tests on our beautiful attempts. Until one day when a bird flew in our second floor fire escape door which was left open because it was a hot summer day. In flew a bird and chaos ensued.

Penmanship Class

It was a hot June day.
Door to fire escape ajar,
In flew a bird
And disrupted

Our perfectly shaped
Letters during
Penmanship class
Under the watchful eye

Of our teacher.
Bird left its dropping
On the girl's desk
In front of me.

A brown paper towel
Cleaned the desk. Students
Screaming and laughing
Watched the bird fly off.

During penmanship classes in Massachusetts, I remember the inkwells were filled with dark black permanent ink. We were supposed to dip our pens in to write. Most of us were on task except for one boy.

Inkwells

My school in
Massachusetts had
Fold top desks
With ink wells.

Dark black, indelible
Ink filled them.
During penmanship
Class, we dipped pens

Into the inkwells.
Not everyone.
One boy was
Busy dipping a

Girl's blond
Braids into the
Inkwell. He got into
Big trouble.

My father claimed I cut my head open on those stone steps leading into my school when I was chasing the boys and my head met the stairs. Since my mother was a nurse, I knew about ether and did not want a local anesthetic the doctor wanted to inject with that long needle into my forehead.

Old Snellville School

Big stone steps
Fourth grade recess
Outside
I chased the boys.

Lost my footing,
Cracked open my
Forehead on the steps,
Cried.

School phoned
My mother who
Walked one mile
From Cedar Street.

To the doctor.
Not wanting the
Shot before stitches,
I screamed for ether.

Saw a merry go round
Vivid blue background.
Mickey Mouse, Donald Duck
Went round and round.

All the time and money invested taking me to Boston to have the gap closed between my front teeth was for naught when I fell from the jungle gym in first grade and broke the teeth. My poor mother.

Much to her Chagrin

I was about five
When my mother,
A registered nurse,
Took me to Boston

For the operation
To close the gap
In my front teeth.
Never bothered me.

Returned home
A gapless smile now.
Didn't bother me.
Then came first grade.

Loved those monkey bars
During recess
Fell from the top
Cracked two front teeth.

I stayed in school.
My mother's cry of dismay
Was worse
Than my new smile.

Probably my mother was not thrilled when my father came home with three kittens for us. She had allergies and so did one of my sisters. We kept the cats outside and in the garage.

Three little Kittens

Our father brought
Home three kittens
For us girls.
Two were tiger

The other black
And white.
Mom was allergic
So they stayed outdoors.

Made beds for
Them in the garage.
Caught mice and
Tossed them in the

Air like rag dolls.
One was run over.
Gave the others away.
Asthma.

The lawn mower had no gasoline engine. A simple one pushed by hand. When my father did our lawn, the frogs woke up and jumped away from the blades. We tried to catch the frogs.

Frogs Jumping

Whenever my Dad
Mowed the lawn
In Sturbridge
With a reel lawn mower

The frogs leapt
And jumped out
Of the way.
We gave chase

And caught some
Of the squirmy
Slimy creatures
And let them go

Again. The stone
Wall my Dad built
Also had snakes
Not our favorites.

There were many snakes, mostly garter snakes where we lived but to a five year old, it was scary.

It Slithered

My mother left my
Youngest sister alone
At home while she
Drove two of us to school.

Frightened, my little
Sister walked
Down the
Road to find us.

A slithering snake
Emerged from
The nearby swamp
And caused her

Alarm. Frozen in fear
She stood crying
Awaiting
Mother's rescue.

We played during long summer days outside our house. One day, sitting in a small patch of low bushes and stones, we talked for hours before we saw it: a snake. We had not disturbed one another until that moment.

Sat with a Friend

On a lazy
Summer day
The three of us
Sat out back

Near the woods
Behind our
Sturbridge home.
We played our

Imaginary games
Speaking quietly
With one another
Very intent on the game.

Suddenly one of us
Spotted the coiled
Creature lazing with
Us. A snake.

First Communions were celebrated in style. I had a fancy white dress, veil, gloves and white silk stockings and white shoes. I was not to get anything dirty before going to church. My father filming us with his 8mm movie camera filmed me jumping over the sidewalk around our house. Good thing I did not fall.

White Silk Stockings

New white shoes
White dress and veil
Garter belt
To hold the

White silk stockings
Turned over at
The top to fit
Her seven year old legs.

Rosary beads
Held in white
Gloved hands.
First Communion today.

Cameras flashing
Adults gushed at
Their offspring
As they processed

Into church led by
Two older girls
Dressed as angels
With wings.

Probably on impulse, my father made arrangements for a new pilot, nineteen years old, to take his girls up in the single engine plane to experience flying. How he convinced our mother, I do not know.

What was Dad thinking?

My mother was
Not thrilled
When Dad said
We could take our

First plane trip
Single engine plane
Nineteen year old
Student pilot.

Her only offspring
Aged nine, seven and
Five would fly alone
Low over our house

On Cedar Street.
Too scared to look out
The window for fear
Of falling out.

We said the people
Waving up to us
Looked like ants
On the ground.

Nothing fancy. No power brakes or steering. Just a plain black bicycle with no seat. To pedal it, we had to stand and that's how we learned to ride the big, black bicycle.

Big, Black Bicycle

I do not recall
If this first bicycle
Had a seat but I
Was too short

To reach the pedals
If I sat in it.
My sisters and I
Learned to ride

This bicycle in the
Backyard over
Uneven ground.
Full concentration

To pedal while
Standing
And not fall.
Smiles when we

Succeeded.
Band aids on knees
And elbows
When we didn't.

Since we did not yet have a television, I went to a neighbor's to watch The Lone Ranger. I recall my hands grasping the chair tightly, my heart pounding and being afraid the first time.

First Time

Invited to a friend's
House. 1950
Was the first time
I ever watched television.

Black and white,
Riveted to the
Small screen watching
The Lone Ranger.

My hands grasped
The armchair tightly
My heart pounded -
Scared.

I knew The Lone Ranger
From radio
But on television
I could SEE him.

I was almost nine when I started piano. Our parents gave us the gift of music which I have passed on to my children as well. Professor LaForce in Massachusetts and Mrs. Hardwick in Colorado were our piano teachers.

Professor LaForce

My first piano teacher
When I was nine
In Massachusetts
Was Professor LaForce.

I learned more than
How to play the piano.
He told stories about
A bullet from the war

Still in his body.
How he made
A church key with
Hot wax in the lock

To play the church organ.
He taught me to play the
William Tell Overture.
A distinguished piano teacher.

In third grade I did not have the feeling I was any good at art after my teacher told us to draw someone sitting under an umbrella at the beach. Apparently my drawing left much to be desired.

Under the Umbrella

Apparently I was
Not good at art
According to my
Third grade teacher.

She told us to
Draw someone sitting
Under an umbrella
At the beach.

Now I could draw
By copying from
An image in front
Of me but

My teacher told
Me it did not
Look right.
Do it over.

I tried to imitate my fourth grade teacher's uncanny ability to write the same with both hands. She never had to move from one end of the board to the other but could write standing in the middle. That was her talent.

Ambidextrous

My fourth grade
Teacher possessed
A unique talent.
She stood in

The middle of the
Big blackboard
In the front and
Began to write

With her left hand
And back to us
And continued not
Moving her spot

With identical
Lettering with
Her right hand.
Ambidextrous.

I remember this house well with gray stained cedar shakes and two fireplaces inside. My father even built us a play house and a big barbeque in the back yard. Stone by stone he assembled the wall out front which still stands there today. Below us was swamp area with blueberry bushes and skunk cabbage. About one mile down the road was the spot where we caught our bus to school for the forty-five minute trip. The Old Sturbridge Village was across the street.

Cedar Street

The house in
Sturbridge on
Cedar Street was
Built by my father.

I remember two
Fireplaces upstairs
And in the basement.
Cedar shakes outside.

Pine doors led to
Secret attic passages
Where we played
On rainy days.

Stone wall out
Front with lots
Of garter snakes
And woods behind us.

My father's father was killed felling trees when our father was only ten and the eldest of six children. They survived hard times and the Depression. One of his younger brothers who never married took care of the rest of the family whenever he could financially. He also had an apple orchard and an abundant garden from which he sold produce. Uncle Joe was a modest, hard working, devout man who had a heart of gold. I will forever remember him with fondness.

Homage to Uncle Joe

My father's brother
An amazing man
Had apple orchards,
Abundant gardens

Fruit trees and
Was a thrifty man
Who never spent on
Himself. He gave

Much of it away to
All his nieces and nephews
To help us with
Education.

He never married
But we were all his
Children. Devout
Catholic, compassionate man.

One thing I loved about Massachusetts and appreciate to this day would have to be the four seasons. We used to play in the piles of colorful leaves in the fall, build snowmen and go sledding in winter, swim in the ponds in summer and plant our gardens in the spring.

Four Seasons

The reasons
I like Massachusetts
And New England
Are the four seasons.

It's hard to say
Which is my
Favorite. Maybe
Fall with all the colors.

As a child, winter
Held magic for
Our wooden sleds
We steered downhill.

Lush, rich greens and
Cold pristine ponds
Bring summer
Memories to me.

I wonder what my mother thought when she got that phone call from her mother a few miles away in Monson? Our mother thought we were out playing with friends in the neighborhood all day. Not so.

Precocious

I was four, my sister two
Still in diapers. I decided
To visit Nana who
Lived two miles away.

Nana had a magical
Player piano. We walked
To visit her one day.
I was careful to look

Both ways when crossing
Streets. Safely there,
Nana phoned our
Mother to ask if

She knew where her
Girls were. Outside playing.
Imagine her shock
To hear us playing the piano.

Being the eldest, I was often accused of being bossy. When illness confined me to inside, I opened the big window and told the neighborhood kids how to play. On a recent trip to the Flynt Avenue home, I discovered that the bush is no longer there, but the house still stands.

Outside My Window

Still recall the
Reddish smoke bush
Outside my window
In Monson.

It must have been
Chicken pox which
Kept me confined
Inside.

A nice, big window
Overlooked the
Yard with the
Smoke bush. From

This vantage point
I could tell the
Neighborhood kids
How to play.

It was a big, old Victorian era house on the top of the hill in Monson. Our parents purchased it for the big sum of four thousand dollars in 1941. Flynt Avenue. I remember the grand piano. My mother said they built the walls around it because that was the only way to get it inside. We left Christmas cookies and milk for Santa on it.

Turn of the Century House

Two maiden aunts
Owned the home
Dating to the 1880s.
My parents purchased

The home when they
Died. No electricity,
No plumbing indoors.
My father renovated

Extensively. It came
With a grand piano
And lots of antique
Furniture.

It was their first
Home. Four thousand.
We could play hide
And seek there.

One of my sisters suffered from asthma as a child, and doctors advised my parents to move somewhere to a better climate for her such as the one found in Colorado. Our parents sold their house and packed belongings to be shipped and moved cross country with no job and no house there. It was a bold move and one borne out of love. My sister no longer had to live in the hospital in the winter.

Oxygen Tent

My sister lay in
The hospital separated
From us by an oxygen
Tent.

Scared and alone
Because of painful
Breathing, the tent
Separated her from us.

Doctors told my
Parents to move
To a different climate
For my sister.

Moved to Colorado
From Massachusetts and
She had no further
Problems with asthma.

About August of 1953 we lived for a few weeks in New Mexico with our Aunt Ellen and Uncle John while our parents went on to California looking for work. They decided on Pueblo, Colorado where they eventually built a house.

Decision Time

Time to move
To Colorado to help
My sister
Breathe easier.

Without a job
My family moved
West to a healthy
Climate. Left us

Briefly in New Mexico
With an Aunt while
Dad looked for a job.
Went to California

Before deciding on
Pueblo, Colorado.
Starting over must
Have been difficult.

The delicate issue of sex education comes to all parents at one point or another. Some prefer the schools to teach it. All my parents did was buy a Catholic-approved book on the subject which did not answer my questions and then later before I married, ask me if there was anything I wanted explained. By that time, no. My father's mother told him not to go into the bushes with the girls. Strange education.

Don't Go Into the Bushes

My Dad often told
Me that when I was
Old enough to understand,
He would explain

More about my questions
About his service during
The War and life issues.
He never did.

By the time I was old enough,
I was no longer
At home and forgot
To ask. He told me

His story of the birds
And the bees: his Polish
Mother told him not to go
Into the bushes with the girls.

When my Aunt and Uncle married in Massachusetts, our mother purchased us matching pink satin dresses with hidden pockets (think they were called Mary Kate dresses) and brown velvet sashes. We looked like triplets although two years apart in age. I remember how everyone danced the polka.

Hidden Pockets

When my aunt and uncle
Married,
My mother bought us
Three special

Pink satin dresses
With hidden pockets
And brown velvet
Sashes at the waist.

Everyone commented
On how cute we looked.
My Polish grandmother
Was all dressed in

Her finest dress
And I marveled at how
She danced the
Polka on the dance floor.

It was normal during and after WWII for soldiers in uniform to hitchhike for rides home. We often picked them up. One time I remember our father taking us to Utica, New York which must have been a long journey in those days. Before that, however, he had hitchhiked there as well. He had a great uncle there whom we met.

Red Handlebar Moustache

We had traveled a long
Distance from Sturbridge
To Utica to visit
Our Great Uncle Stanley.

My father took us
Into the smoke filled
Room -
A corner bar?

I don't recall much
Except his
Moustache
Which was bushy

Red and curled
Up on the ends
A handlebar moustache
Which moved when he laughed.

In the swamp below our house in Sturbridge, Massachusetts, there was plenty of poison ivy, skunk cabbage and blueberries as well as snakes.

Skunk Cabbage

Walking the mile down
Our rural Massachusetts
Road to catch the
School bus,

We had to walk past
A swampy area
Covered with skunk cabbage
And blueberries.

Battling the stinky plant
To get to the blueberries
Was tricky and off
Limits to us.

Abundant poison ivy
Thrived in this
Environment. More
Than once I paid the price.

It is not easy being the second born in the family. My sister found she could frighten and intimidate me by pulling off the legs of Daddy Long Legs spiders and then pick them up, still twitching, and chase after me as I screamed in fear of these creatures.

Daddy Long Legs

My sister knew
My fear of spiders
And would chase
Me around the yard

Holding a twitching
Leg she had
Removed from
The Daddy Long Legs.

It was always
An amusement
To her to even
The score since

She was younger
Than I by two years.
To this day, I
Do not like this arachnid.

COLORADO CHATS

Water is often scarce in Colorado and we were only permitted to water lawns every other day based upon our house number. One day when my sister moved the hose, she found a very long snake in the yard since we lived near the prairie which had rattle snakes. Later my father was sad when he found out he had needlessly harmed the snake.

Time to Move the Hose

Another stifling hot
Summer day in Pueblo.
Odd side of the street
So we could water

The lawn today.
Twelve hours of
Moving the hose
From spot to spot.

Dad was tired
Now so asked
My sister
To move the hose.

Startled shrieks
Six foot bull snake
In the front yard.
Time for the ax.

When we first moved west from Massachusetts, there were frequent dust storms. And even though windows and storm windows were shut, the dirt found its way inside the house. In the fall, the wind whipped up the tumbleweeds which bounced everywhere.

Tumbleweeds

Bouncing, tumbling,
Whirling, zigzagging,
Across the windswept,
Arid earth.

These weeds
Protruding through
Cracked, parched
Hard ground with

Roots searching
For moisture.
And despairing
When rains

Remain scarce,
The loosened weeds
Now rampantly roar
Across the prairie.

Engulfed in anger,
These tumbleweeds
Rage and
Wander aimlessly.

My blue-eyed blond sister frequently wore her hair with braids.

Long Blond Braids

My younger sister
Had long blond
Braids like
Annie Oakley.

So when we
Saw the real one
At the State Fair,
We visited her

Behind the grandstand
Where the rodeo
Took place.
She took one look

At my sister's
Braids and declared
Them
Prettier than hers.

I recall my mother talking about this incident at the Colorado State Fair. It seems that the cowboy had had too much to drink and fell off his horse during his singing performance.

Cowboy Performer

Gene Autry came
To sing his
Cowboy songs
At our State Fair

One August.
We got more
Than we bargained
For when

He fell off
His horse in
The middle of
Grandstand

Because he
Had been
Drinking
My mother said.

Sibling rivalry was alive and well in our Colorado household. All we needed to add to this was a piano piece performed by three of us at the same time and seated on the same piano bench. A recipe for disaster was underway.

Never Ever

We learned the
Hard way that
Having more than
One person

Sitting on the
Piano bench to
Perform a song,
Simply did not work.

The three of us
Sisters and
Friends most days
Did not like this.

Six hands at the
Piano was unique
Or so our parents
And teacher thought.

It was torture
Most times to sit
Next to one another
Much less to play.

We had to wear Western wear when we moved to Colorado. Just like the natives. Or so we thought. It was fun to have long swirling square dance skirts adorned with rick rack.

Fancy Duds

We were transplants
From the East
Out here in the
Colorado prairie.

We donned
Western wear
Just like the
Natives.

Cowboy hats,
Swirling skirts
Adorned with
Rick rack.

Even had caps
In our Western
Pistols which
Made popping noises.

We had left
Familiar Massachusetts
For the wild West
And loved it!

There was nothing quite like ice cold root beer served in frosted mugs like they did at the local root beer stand.

Frosted Mugs

The waitress came
Out to our car
To get our order
Of root beer

In frosted mugs
Which were served
On a tray which
Attached to our car.

We gulped it down
Fast on hot summer
Days at this
Root beer stand.

This was a great
Treat for us.
We piled quickly
Into the car.

It was fascinating to watch the gas stations at war with one another. Each lowered the price per gallon by one cent. The one across the street did the same and threw in a free glass to attract customers.

Former Days

I recall the days
Of gas wars
When one station
Lowered prices

To eighteen cents.
Across the street
Seventeen with
Free glasses.

Then sixteen and
A free loaf of
Bread. Sometimes when
A new bank opened

There were free
T-shirts to each
Customer. So
Dad made us get

In the car
For these free
Articles of clothing.
We didn't understand.

Members of a local 4H club called the Bonnie Belles of Belmont after our subdivision in Pueblo, we each had different projects on an annual basis. First year foods included making muffins from scratch and by hand. No electric mixers were allowed, not even the year we made cakes.

Muffins

Our father loved
The year in 4H when
We made muffins
As our food project.

He came into
The kitchen to tell
Us how good
They smelled.

Every day
The same
Recipe for
Twelve muffins.

Every day the
Same comments.
He lavished us
With his praise.

I went through his line every day for lunch and paid for it at his cash register. He was a senior and I a sophomore when he asked me to his prom. With only two days to spare, I announced I was going to the prom. My poor mother was up all night sewing me the most beautiful prom dress with bunches of pink flowers on it.

Short Notice

The year I was a
High school sophomore,
A senior boy at the
Cafeteria checkout

At school got the
Courage to ask
Me to the prom.
When I announced

That at home, my
Mother smiled and
Said she would make
My dress.

She had to stay up
All night sewing
Because the prom
Was the next day.

My parents had decided without telling me that I would not be allowed to date until I was sixteen. There was heated, whispered discussion out of earshot when I said a boy had asked me to go swimming at the local country club one block away and in his car. Imagine a girl in a one piece bathing suit at age fifteen. I was permitted and felt as if I had broken barriers for my younger sisters.

Not Yet

She's only fifteen
My mother said.
She can't go out
Alone on a date

With a boy
In a car until
She is sixteen.
My parents huddled

To discuss the
Dilemma when I
Asked if I could go
To the country club

Pool during the
Afternoon. They
Finally consented.
Grownup freedom.

Year six in food preparation in 4-H meant preparing a meal for four with a budget of two dollars and fifty cents and within four hours from setup to cooking, to serving and to cleaning up afterward. In a glass enclosed kitchen for all to view. At eighteen and a high school senior, I won the Colorado Grand Championship and a trip to Chicago as part of my prize. I never took that trip, opting instead to do my exams in school which could have been made up at a later date. I was allowed to make that decision.

Purple Ribbon

Glass enclosed kitchen
For four hours at the
Fairgrounds to cook
A meal for four

With $2.50 allotted.
Waldorf Salad
Liver a la Creole
Sweet potato

Lemon fluff for
Dessert. The judge
Came to check our time
Charts and award points.

The Colorado 4H Grand
Championship for Food
Preparation went to me.
A big purple ribbon.

Home-made bread from scratch mixed and kneaded and allowed to rise twice before baking was at least a weekly ritual the year we made yeast bread in 4-H. I also had to do bread demonstrations because I had won at the county level.

Yeast Bread

The year I made
Yeast bread from
Scratch for 4-H
Rivaled the muffin year.

Dad watching me
Knead the dough.
Mouth already
Watering for the taste.

He could hardly
Wait for it
To bake in the
Oven. Ah the smell.

It reminded him
Of the Polish bakery
In Massachusetts
Where he went

As a boy and
Bought
Fresh bread and
Cheese Danish.

We often had wonderful cakes and pies our mother made from scratch for her family. Sometimes the results were better than other times.

Waste Not

Near Thanksgiving
One year, our mother
Baked a pumpkin
Pie. She made good pies.

Most of the time.
Today however, it
Tasted awful to us.
You see, there was

No sugar in it.
Not wanting to
Waste all her
Efforts, our mother

Simply added sugar
To the baked pie
And stirred.
It was delicious.

My mother had inadvertently switched her two pans of water this day. One was for rice and the other for her instant coffee.

Don't Switch Pans

One Sunday dinner
With a roast,
Vegetables and
Rice,

We complained
Loudly that
The rice tasted
Horrible.

There was no
Salt in it.
Our mother then
Exclaimed:

That's why my coffee
Tasted terrible
Today. It had salt in it.
Switched pans of water.

When I finish using a pan, it is my habit to put some soapy water in it to soak before I wash it. This gave new meaning to the expression to wash one's mouth with soap.

By Accident

When I am cooking
And done with a
Pan, I normally
Let the pan soak

In soapy water.
Today with fresh
Vegetables from the
Garden, we

Anticipated a gourmet
Treat except
For the fact
That I had accidently

Switched pans and now
Had a mouthful of
Vegetables cooked
In soapy water.

In the 1950s when gas was inexpensive and cars large and ugly looking, it was the "in thing" on a Friday night to drag the gut which meant mindlessly driving around and around the same city block to show off who was in the car with you and the car of course. Teens enjoying themselves.

Dragging the Gut

Downtown Pueblo
On a Saturday night
Teens drove in
Their cars

Round and round
The block.
Flashy cars and
Ones with fins.

It was the thing
To do in the fifties:
To see and
Be seen.

We called it
Dragging the gut.
Parents didn't
Understand their teens.

Gas didn't cost
Much back then.
Girls and guys
Having some fun.

Entertainment in the 1950s usually revolved around drive-in movies which began fashionably late so that teens got to stay up later than usual and be with their friends.

Drive-in Movies

About the only form
Of weekend entertainment
Was going to the drive-in
Movies with friends.

Drove in and parked
On an incline for
The best view of the
Giant screen.

Rolled down the
Windows to get
The scratchy
Speaker to

Attach to the
Window to
Get sound.
Cuddle up.

During my freshman year of college, I worked in the dorm cafeteria serving food and picking up the trays afterwards. I did this for three meals daily and on weekends. In return, my room and board was paid for. It seems that we had this certain meat every Friday dubbed mystery meat because no one knew what kind of meat it was.

Mystery Meat

Food in the college
Dorm was the usual
Dull fare of
Mounds of mashed potatoes

Loads of gravy
Canned vegetables.
Starving students
Would eat anything

Except the Friday
Menu which included
Mystery meat.
So called

Because we didn't
Know what kind it was.
Chew and chew
And finally swallow the lump.

Sunday mornings my father wound up the one hundred year old German music box with metal records. It chimed sweet melodies as we arose and readied ourselves for church.

Getting Ready for Church

Sunday mornings when
My father arose
He cranked up
The antique German

Music box with
Metal records.
Melodious tones
Rang through the house.

No alarm clock was
Necessary. This
Was a gentle way
To wake up the

Household of girls
And his wife.
His harem
He lovingly called us.

Re-runs of the Lawrence Welk Show can still be viewed. One of the musical groups on the program included the Little Lennon Sisters. When we sang at church, our priest called us his little Lennon sisters as well.

The Niemczura Sisters

The priest referred
To us as his little
Lennon sisters like
On the Lawrence Welk

Television show.
I played the church organ
And we sang
For daily Mass

And three times on
Sundays and for all
The weddings and
Funerals.

From age thirteen to
Age eighteen, I did
This with my sisters.
Then off to college.

As the church organist, I had to select music and was doing so regarding music to have for the next Sunday. Our younger sister finally blurted out as only a four year old can and asked why we didn't have any hers and only "hims." We tried to explain this difficult concept.

Church Music

She, the youngest,
Overheard the
Discussion
About which

Hymns to
Play for church
On Sunday.
She often

Felt left out
Of our conversations
As the youngest
So we

Heard her ask
Why?
Why aren't there
Any hers?

And only
"Hims"?
Hard to explain
To a four year old.

For two years when I was in seventh and eighth grades, I begged my parents to allow us to go to parochial school because of the public school's reputation. I can't say I learned much during those two years and was glad to go back to public school.

Erasers

When she was annoyed
With us, the nun
Threw erasers.
Behind her back

She was called battle ax
In whispered tones.
To stay one step
Ahead of her wrath

And to teach her a
Lesson, we eighth
Graders passed
Blank notes

Which she couldn't
Read aloud to the
Class. We smiled.
The joke was on her.

One time on a visit to the East coast when my mother must have been in her seventies, I recall an odd thing she said about aging. She said it was the pits. I didn't understand at the time but do today. With all the accompanying aches and pains, aging can be the pits.

Aging is the Pits

Startled when
My mother said
That aging is
The pits,

I fathomed
To understand
What she
Meant.

I did not yet
Have gray hair
And arthritis
And other ailments.

Now I understand.
I walk with a
Cane and do
Stretching exercises.

Our red delicious apple tree in our backyard in Pueblo was never sprayed because our father discovered a robin's nest with little birds in it. He was mindful and careful of these birds every year. I imagine the apples must have been good though.

No Spraying

The red delicious
Apple tree had
Heavy limbs from
All the apples.

There was a robin's
Nest in the tree.
My father
Decided not to

Spray the tree
But to let the
Apples fall to
The grass below.

He protected the
Birds as he did us.
Boy Scouts picked up
The apples to feed horses.

Sometimes it was annoying to always be told and reminded of thinking about outcomes or better ways to do things. Life with an engineer can be that way.

Engineer's Daughter

Early in life
I learned from my
Dad that there
Was a better way

To do things.
He was an engineer
And trained to look
For better, more

Productive ways
To do things.
Efficiency was his
Buzzword.

Sometimes I tired
Of being told there
Was a better way
To load the dishwasher.

One visit East my father commented to my husband that there was probably only one way to load the dishwasher. He knew the way I had been taught. My husband said he knew that way. My right-handed brain knew that way and my husband's left-handed brain knew differently.

It Defied Logic

There is only one
Way to properly
Load our dishwasher
Which was taught

Me by my father,
The engineer.
Use logic he told
Me as he

Demonstrated the
Correct way -
Correct as he perceived
It that is.

My husband's
Left-handed mind had
A different way
Which defied logic.

What a welcome I received when I was introduced to my new fifth grade class in Colorado.

All Good Things Come in Threes

When we moved to
Colorado from Massachusetts
I was in fifth grade.
The teacher introduced

Me to the class
As Mary Ann
And the class
Groaned in unison.

Taken aback and
Somewhat insulted
I was unsure what
To think of them.

You see, there
Were two others
Named Mary Ann.
I made three!

Load upon load of sand was transported via wheelbarrow by our father from front to backyard for his new workshop. Fourteen hour days of heavy labor were involved.

Wheelbarrow

My father wanted
To build a small
Workshop in our
Backyard to

Create his wooden
Furniture. Had
One ton of dirt
Dumped in our

Colorado driveway.
Wheelbarrow loads
Were transported
During fourteen hour

Days of back-breaking work.
Mixed with cement, the
Dirt would form the foundation.
Ever the thrifty man

He chose to do things
Himself. Unlike my Dad, I
Hire to have snow removed
From our driveway.

Ever protective of his children and grandchildren, my father made an angry phone call to the roofers who had put a new roof on the home after a hail storm. But they dropped nails in the lawn where our son stepped in his flip flops.

Hopping Mad

My father was
Hopping mad in
Colorado when our
Son stepped into the lawn

To give Grandpa a
Hug and a nail
Went through his
Flip flop and into his foot.

Howling and crying
Our son sat on the lawn
Pulled off the flip flop
And removed the nail.

Grandpa was on the
Phone to the roofers
Who had replaced the
Roof again after a

Colorado hail storm.
Grandpa spewed forth an
Ear-piercing volley of
Unrepeatable words.

All of us continued piano lessons with Mrs. Hardwick in Pueblo. We were required to practice one hour per day. My parents had to soon add a second piano to the basement of our house so that we all had time to do our required practice. When I was advanced enough, I was expected to practice four to six hours daily in the summer. Usually two or three hours later, I could no longer sit and practice.

The Hardwick Music Studio

When we moved to Pueblo,
Mrs. Hardwick gave us
Piano lessons. Our mother
Observed in a rocking chair.

We were expected to
Practice one hour
Daily and
As we progressed,

A second piano was added.
One upstairs, one downstairs.
Music drifted out all
Our windows in summer.

We even played a piece
Composed for six hands
And performed at recitals
My talented sisters and I.

We played this song in the 4-H talent show and won a ribbon. We played for recitals. It was a novelty. But we did not enjoy it and were quite happy when we no longer had to do this.

Six Hands at the Piano

We barely fit
On the piano bench
And we were supposed
To practice the piece.

She keeps hitting
My arm. I don't have
Enough room. Our
Mother cajoled.

Count, girls,
Remember to count.
Played impromptu at the
Broadmoor and got

Candy bars from a patron.
Wisely, only one time with
Six hands at the piano.
Never again.

I learned to dance the twist my first year of college. When I came home and showed my parents at Christmas what I had learned, my father's only comment was that I might throw my back out if I danced that way too long.

Learning Experience

Going off to college
Was a great learning
Experience.
I returned at Christmas

To show off some
New found knowledge
And demonstrated
The Twist.

With hips swaying
And knees twisting
Back and forth,
I danced to the music.

My father laughed
And cautioned me
Not to throw out
My back.

This poem is about an April Fool's Day trick played on our class by our teacher. He did it without missing a beat until the end of class.

Dumbfounded

We were in his
Ninth grade advanced
Algebra class.
We sensed

Something
Different today.
The wall clock was
Upside down.

We became frustrated
When he refused to look
At the clock despite our
Repeated pleas.

The bell rang at
The end of class
When he said
April Fool's Day to us.

Surrounded by all his women in the family, I never heard my father swear until the time we had to stand on the saw horse to hold up the heavy sheetrock panels above our head for the basement ceiling.

New Words

My father liked to
Build things and
Finished the basement
In our Colorado home

On Horseshoe Drive.
Four of us stood on
The sawhorse and
Held heavy sheetrock
Panels above our heads

For the ceiling. Hammer in
Hand my father swung a
Heavy blow
Intended for the nail

But missed and hit
His thumb instead.
That day we learned some
New words I can't repeat here.

MUSINGS FROM UPSTATE NEW YORK

When our daughter is away on a trip, my husband has the short straw and takes care of her cats.

Cat Duty

Got the short straw again.
Walked this morning
Breakfast and shopping.
Then cat duty.
Feline zoo.

Await my visit.
Food.
Big fat cat
Eats for two.
Hiding under the sofa

The shy one
Waits for me to
Shove food underneath.
Feline felicity
Cat Duty.

Off Cat Duty

The cat mistress
Returns from her trip
Today.
I feel elated.

No more searching
For the timid one
Who hides under
The sofa.

Watching that
The fat one
Only gets her portion
Of the food.

Never certain
She does.
Still I miss
My feline zoo.

Poems from the Track in the Wee Hours

I encountered many strange creatures as I walked the high school track nearby in the wee hours of the morning between 4-5 AM. One such morning a skunk approached and I wondered if I was going to be able to drive back home if I got sprayed. I held my breath and kept walking and praying at the same time.

Skunk

Black and White
Striped
Meandering
Across my path.

Panic sets in
What if
This creature
Sprays?

No.
We go about our
Business.
Ignore
One another.

I often composed poetry in my head as I walked the high school track. The action of walking triggered memories in my brain. My father's birthday was in November so in the fall, I often thought of him as I walked.

Frozen Silence

Frost this morning
On the track.
Hides my tears.

Remembering him
This November morning.
Gone some time now.

Miss him in this
Stillness.
Frozen Silence.

I was on my first Fulbright in Germany with our two young children, 3 and 6 years old when I got a letter from my father that he was dying of cancer. Crowded into a phone booth in the small village in Germany, I phoned him and kept feeding the phone every 20 seconds to be able to continue our conversation. We both cried and our children wanted to know what was wrong. The last thing my father said during this conversation in late September was that he would wait for my return the following July. He died less than one month later on October 18, 1990. He told me not to come home to the US for a funeral but to stay in Germany. I abided by his wishes as hard as it was for me.

Just died

Got the news
Today.
He died.

Didn't wait
For me to return.
Grief and sadness.

Sang Amazing Grace
In the tiny German chapel
In English.

And thought of
My father
With loving sadness.

Inspiration for the next two came from a friend's experiences in Texas with a visiting dog in the neighborhood who bothered his horse.

Uninvited Guest

A visitor
Again.
Herds the horse.
Nuisance.

Why does this dog
Visit me?
Herds me
To action?

Not in
This heat
Of the Texas
Sun.

Back inside
Until later
When the uninvited
Visitor returns.

Where is
His home?
Maybe
Here with me.

Another Scorcher

Out early to
Pull weeds.
My new hobby.
Dandelions multiply

Faster than I
Can pull them.
Cowgirl beckons;
Herds Tish again!

Already hot and
Tired. The day
Is young still.
Walk Heidi and Max II.

No golf today.
Must hide inside
Until night approaches.
Another Texas scorcher.

Searching for a spot to recharge the batteries before another teaching year, I met with one of my sisters in Sedona, Arizona to rest and explore.

Beauty and Warmth

All the stress
Leaves my body
As I gaze around
Awestruck.

The red rock
Formations loom
All around.
Beauty pervades

My eyes.
My soul is calm.
Such a wondrous
Landscape

This Sedona.
Hot sun, blue skies
Radiate warmth
Inside and out.

In conversation with a colleague, I discovered he had had a similar experience to the one we had with our daughter when we were at the doctor's for a routine exam. We both had a good laugh. The nurse was concerned for Ethan yesterday at his physical in terms of the vision test. He repeatedly said that he couldn't do the letter chart only to find out that he was trying to read the lines as whole words. How would a seven-year-old pronounce "FDZGHJ"?

Routine Eye Exam

It was a routine eye
Exam when the
Nurse uncovered a
Problem with

Our seven year old
Son. Having
Already mastered
The alphabet

And having learned to
Sound out words, he
Read above grade
Level we were told.

Now he had
Difficulty trying to
Read the eye chart
Word: FDZGHJ

Our children became fluent in German during my Fulbright year near Stuttgart. Upon returning to the US, however, and at a subsequent eye exam, the nurse was concerned about my daughter's vision. She was told to identify the pictures on the chart which she did correctly and in German. So I had to go in to interpret for her.

Eye Chart

Our three year old
Had difficulty
Identifying the
Pictures on the

Eye chart
To check her vision.
The nurse took her
In alone and

Returned to tell
Me there was a
Problem with saying
Correct object names.

Puzzled, I went in
To help. Emily
Identified everything
Perfectly.

In German.
I interpreted. You see
We had just come
Back from one year in Germany.

Children often have simple solutions to problems like the time we were short of ready cash at home.

Solution to the Problem

Our son about four
Playing with toy cars
Overheard my husband
And me asking one another

If we had any money
At home. Since we
Had none,
He offered us

His best advice
In youthful tones:
Drive to the
Supermarket and

Just ask the
Checkout lady
For some; she always
Gives people money.

I wrote this about my friend when dementia entered her life and she could no longer understand why she had to be in assisted living when she owned two homes of her own.

I Am There Now

We worked together
My friend and I.
Then she retired
But we stayed in touch.

Some time ago
She told me she
Had dementia.
As calmly as if she

Had a cold.
Assisted living
Came next along
With not understanding

Why she has to live
Elsewhere. Her friends
Are here and she
Is there.

My friend has dementia now but gave me this wonderful recipe and shared fresh collards from her garden with me. When we have little to talk of, we can always talk about how good these collards are.

Collards

I learned about a
Good collard recipe
From a librarian friend
Of mine.

Olive oil, garlic
Over medium heat.
Wash and tear the greens
Off the thick stems.

Discard the stems.
Cook in chicken broth
For about three hours
And serve as soup.

A giant boost of vitamins
And energy
This green soup.
A family favorite.

My husband tries to outsmart the rabbits who like his garden. I watch the various sized rabbits in our suburban lawn. One day they were all lined up outside the garden fence drooling and trying to figure out a way inside to the tasty vegetable morsels.

Under the Apple Trees

Out front under
Our apple trees
We have resident
Visitors.

They pay homage
To the clover and weeds
And relish the shade
Of the trees.

The garden fence
Was erected
Because of these
Friends of ours.

They like to
Eat us out of
House and home
These rabbits.

A long-time friend of mine and I like to get away from the daily hustle and bustle of life and take a mini-vacation to a well-manicured small town nearby. Homes are set back from the street and reminiscent of those in New England with sidewalks and large shade trees. The small restaurant, Ebeneezer's Café, features a half sandwich, cup of soup and homemade pie for dessert. It is a cozy place to relax and renew friendships.

Gone Gathering

We were on one
Of our gathering
Trips. My friend and I.
Like our ancestors

Before us who hunted,
Fished and gathered.
We relished these
Mini-vacations together.

Just the two of us
Talking, laughing,
Shopping and going
Out to lunch together

In a nearby city.
Cup of soup, a half
Sandwich and pie.
Worries left behind us.

My artist's eye sees things differently. The only reason I went along on such shopping trips was because I held the plastic money. I was not fond of the loud rock music emanating from the store. So my daughter was mortified when I spied the pony tail holders and declared them for their intended purpose: buttons for my latest fleece jacket I was sewing. She was fearful others would know my ignorance.

Things Are Not as They Appear Sometimes

Things are not always as they
Appear or are intended.
With me. I view things
Differently, you see.

Take the pretty
Round felt multicolored
Balls attached to elastic
I spied while

Shopping for clothes
With my teenage
Daughter who
Was mortified when

I loudly declared
What beautiful buttons.
Oh, Mom, they're
Pony tail holders.

As my children grew up, they heard Mom's stories of teaching which my husband patiently listened to. Now it is my turn to listen as our daughter goes through nursing school.

Love's Duty

The first duty
Of love is to
Listen
So I practice

Each time
Our nursing student
Daughter has
A litany of complaints.

She learned from
The master of complaints.
I was a teacher who
Had lots of stories

And complaints at the
Dinner table.
Listening takes
Patience. So too love.

I am convinced that everyone must know a workaholic. This is written for all the workaholics I know and who need a vacation but don't realize they do.

In a Hurry

He was always
In a hurry
To do more things
Than his day would

Permit.
He was a workaholic
Incapable of slowing
Down to realize

What he had done
To his family
Who bravely hurried
About their lives too.

He slept poorly
And needed to hurry
To take a long overdue
Rest from hurrying.

In our busy lives, we often leave one another a note as a reminder of something to do. This was the inspiration for this poem.

Another Note

Lying on the kitchen
Table is another
Note from him.
Referee tonight.

Will need to eat
Early.
Cryptic
But conveyed

The necessary
Details of dinner.
Now I have
Noticed our

Daughter also
Leaves notes
For herself
Reminders to study.

As our children grew and were busy at the computer or doing homework, we often heard them say to "hold on" when we called them to dinner.

Hold On

Not wanting to
Be interrupted
With tasks at
Hand,

Our son was
Wont to say
Hold on
Frequently.

As he grew
Older and used
The computer
More often.

Exasperated when
He didn't come
To dinner right away,
It simply grew cold.

I think of my children as frozen in time at one certain age when I know full well they have grown up now. It's the same with children of our friends. They remain the same as when we last saw them. Maybe we're the ones who grew old.

Hidden Life

Uncertain at what
Precise moment in
Time it happens,
They grow old

In front of our
Eyes. Quite
Suddenly. Little
Boy one day

Moody teen the
Next. Young adult
Out of school and
Married.

His life hidden
From mine now.
Why didn't I see
This happen?

My children recall vividly to this day of the time I drove them to piano lessons in nearby Phoenix, NY. A blizzard had cancelled all schools. The snow may have closed school but not piano lessons. Was I in my right mind to drive there? If you asked my two, they would verify that I was crazy.

To Piano in a Blizzard

My children will
Never let me forget
The time I drove them
To piano in a blizzard.

School had been cancelled
Because of the snow
Blowing, drifting.
I phoned ahead

To ask how the
Weather was in the
Next town before I
Drove them to piano.

It had cleared so
We drove to lessons -
Loud, indignant complaints
From the back seat.

As parents we watch our adult children make life's choices and pray that they make good ones.

Yearnings

Maybe she is
Afraid to be
Alone which is
Why she seeks

Out the company
Of friends.
We worry that
She has narrowed

Her choice of
Companions by
Being with him.
Their worlds

Are vastly different
But they are attracted
To each other.
We pray.

Not finding a neighborhood friend to play with on a particular day, our daughter was overheard telling a friend that she could always ask her Dad to play if no one else was around. As soon as a friend appeared, it was another matter and Dad was easily discarded.

Next Best

Our social butterfly
Sought constant
Play time with the
Neighborhood kids.

Sometimes when
Playmates were in
Short supply,
Our daughter told

Her friends, they
Could always
Ask their Dad to
Play with

Them. Until the
Next friend came
Along. Then it was
Bye, Dad.

Everyone knew this slow, lazy postal clerk who whistled. He knew he was close to retirement and cared not that his lines were agonizingly slow. Colleagues picked up the slack as they rolled their eyes. I used to drive to another post office in the village because I could make the ten minute drive back and forth and be done with my mailing before I would be waited on by the slowpoke in his post office.

The Whistler

The post office
Line is slow
As molasses in
January.

I determine the
Cause to be
The clerk who
Engages in

Small talk
While we wait.
Other clerks
Handle three

Times the customers.
I know his presence
Since he always
Whistles.

Kindred spirits, the customer and I smiled at one another and commented on the lovely canes we were using. They were identical, multi-colored with a paisley print.

Two Canes

We met at
The supermarket
And smiled
Immediately.

I guess you
Could call us
Twins
Since we walked

With identically-
Colored canes.
Multi-colored paisley
Worn curves from

Years of use.
We became instant
Friends with
Two canes.

As I faced shoulder surgery and recall my mother's words about aging, this poem came to mind.

Parts Wear Out

Years of pulling the white
Screens up and down
For the class and
Writing on chalkboards

Have taken
Their toll now.
Shoulder surgery
To repair damage.

My mother always
Said that the
Aging process
Is the pits.

I thought
That negative of her
But now fully
Comprehend.

TEACHING EXPERIENCES

After forty-six years experience teaching, I have many stories. Some are from teaching in the U.S. and some from Germany. The next one was written after a grueling year with a new evaluation system in place known as APPR. This was introduced to New York State during the 2012-13 school year.

I teach

Their eyes follow me.
Furtive glances.
Questions and
Aha moments.

Storytelling
Chalk to the board
Laughter smiles and
Some frowns.

These are my children.
This is their future.
Politicians take
Away time for trivia.

Don't they know
What they're doing
To all of us?
Long for former times.

One morning after walking, I was driving home from the local high school track when the lights of an oncoming car blinded me forcing me to the right shoulder. I lowered my window, and the police officer asked me one word "newspaper" since he thought that only people who deliver newspapers would be out at this hour of the AM.

Who goes there?

Driving home
Before sunrise,
After walking,
Blinded by the lights.

Forced off
The right shoulder,
A policeman
Stopped me.

Newspaper?
No, teacher.
I walk
Before school.

End of
Discussion.
Drove home
Smiling all the way.

I wrote this in my classroom with no students and after I heard of my sister-in-law's cancer. These feelings needed words so I wrote this poem. The sea of souls refer to my students in class.

Alone

Alone I sit amidst a sea of souls
Casting a glance at the rain-swept
Landscape, trees swaying in the
Sweltering heat.

Why, I wonder, am I lost
In the sea of souls,
Alone in my thoughts,
Barely feeling?

Trying to fathom
What it all means
What the reasons?
Why? - lost.

Again and alone
Amidst the sea of souls
Who know not.
Can't understand.

My pain, my pent up
Tears, emotions spill
Forth; alone again
Alone amidst the sea of souls.

During the 1990-91 school year, I was a Fulbright Exchange Teacher in Neresheim at a comprehensive school where I taught grades 6-10. I had a 7th grade class of Hauptschule students destined to be blue collar workers. They would finish formal schooling after 9th grade and begin apprenticeships such as auto mechanics. They knew they were not to swear in class, but I was the new kid on the block. We had been told to speak only English so these students assumed I knew no German. There was also an 18 yr. old in this class. When I uttered *"Du kommst zum Arrest, wenn es so weiter geht."* the student turned bright red. I had told him the equivalent of he would be under arrest if he continued to talk that way.

Never Again

The new year found
Me teaching in Germany.
Fond of using their
Dialects, the students

Thought I would not
Understand their
Swear words
Forbidden in class.

One bold seventh
Grade boy spewed forth
A streak of vulgarity.
Imagine his utter shock

When I responded with a
Stern warning in German.
His face turned many
Shades of brilliant crimson.

Riesstr. 26

Schweindorf

During my first Fulbright year, we lived in a wonderful village called Schweindorf. Our hosts became our second family. They owned a big farmhouse which housed a restaurant and living quarters. Hilde and Horst were the best parents for my two children the year I taught in Germany.

Our Second Family

There was always
A terrific noon meal
Ready and waiting
When I returned

From teaching in
The Comprehensive
School in Neresheim.
Hilde made a hot soup,

Meat, and tasty
Swabian *Spaetzle*.
She loved our two
Children as her own.

We shared in
Family celebrations
And became immersed
In German culture.

During 1994-95 I was selected to be a Fulbright Exchange Teacher to Berlin, Germany. We lived in a Communist-era apartment building with a crumbling red stone exterior. The elevator frequently was out of order to our 11th floor apartment.

The Golden House

This school year found
Me in Eastern Berlin
Teaching high school.
Our temporary home

For the year was
In a high rise apartment
Dubbed the "Golden House"
And built when the

Communists were in
Power. The exterior
Embedded with small red stones
Had been a former showcase.

Like the government,
The red stone exterior
Also crumbled onto
The balcony.

German Living and School Experiences

I taught as a Fulbright Exchange Teacher in Germany from 1990-91 and 1994-95, the first time in Neresheim, near Stuttgart and the second time in Berlin. Our two children went along and attended German schools which were inspiration for these next few poems.

Stefan

Big for his age
And chubby
This second grade boy
In Berlin

Had a crush on
My second grade
Daughter who
Had no interest

In this loudmouth
Boy who shouted
Hallo, Emilie
Across the trolley

Tracks as we were
Boarding the trolley
To the city. She shook
Her head in disgust.

Somewhat shocked, I discovered after the fact that my daughter's second grade class in Berlin had been taught sex education. She arrived home with the illustrated paperback book from school. I tried not to show her my reaction since it was just another book to her about a topic well above her head. She knew enough, however, that it must have been something forbidden by reactions from classmates. We still have the book on our shelf: *Peter, Ida und Minimum*.

Sex Education

Unaware that our
Daughter would receive
Sex education in second
Grade complete with

An age-appropriate
Illustrated paperback
Book to read, I
Was shocked that I had

Not been informed
Ahead of time.
The cat was out of the
Bag.

Things were done
Differently in this
Elementary school in
Berlin, Germany.

Taken aback by the teaching methods employed by the swim teacher at the elementary school in Berlin, I quietly and quickly obtained a doctor's note to excuse our daughter from any future classes. I was not going to take on the German education system with this one. Besides the pools had too much chlorine for her.

Swim Lesson

It was an understatement
To say I was shocked
By my daughter's tale
Of utter fear from

Her swim lesson
With her second grade
Class in Berlin, Germany.
My daughter related how

The teacher threw into the pool
Those timid or fearful
Of going into the water.
My daughter included.

Quick to act and
Rectify this perceived wrong,
I marched to the doctor's office
For the note excusing my

Daughter from swim lessons
For the remainder of her
Year in Germany.
She learned to swim at home.

When I took our two children to Germany for both of my Fulbright teaching experiences, Tom and Emily attended German schools. Emily was in kindergarten the first time, when I got a message from the teacher that there was a problem. It seems our daughter was playing by herself in the room. I explained patiently that this was a new country, a new culture and language and that I was confident our daughter would soon be right at home.

My Little Native Speakers

Learning a foreign language
At an early age is
Child's play and
Very natural.

In two short months
Our daughter learned
The German language.
She adjusted to her

New surroundings in
The German village
And became confident.
No one suspected that

She was an American.
Young minds are like
Sponges absorbing
The language.

We attended the wedding of one of the daughters of our second family in Germany in a fairy tale castle in a small Bavarian town. It was magical for our two who were now 16 and 12 to return to Germany and visit with family and friends and to celebrate the wedding.

Fairy Tale Wedding

In a small Bavarian
Castle surrounded
By friends and family
From around the world,

The happy couple
Married. Picture perfect
Day. Abundant food
And beverage,

Guests sang and
Danced all day
And all night.
An Oktoberfest band

Performed. Breakfast in
Another Bavarian
Town. Forever in
Our memory.

Our son received a guinea pig for his seventh birthday when we were in Schweindorf, Germany. He named it Mike after Michelangelo, one of the popular group called the Turtles. At the end of our Fulbright year, Mike traveled to the U.S. to live with us for about nine years.

Mike - a Love Story

He came to Tom's
Life on his seventh
Birthday in Germany.
This brown and black

Long furry-haired
Creature who
Hailed from Koesingen,
Home of Oscar Meyer.

For the time
And money spent
To bring Mike home,
Twenty guinea pigs

Might have been
Purchased. But who
Would take beloved
Mike away from Tom?

My colleague Joe in technology education and I formed an interdisciplinary project in which he taught 6th graders how to make wooden toys, and I taught them the German they needed since they had new vocabulary to learn in technology education. We toured a local German toy factory as part of the project.

The German Toyshop

Putting his black metal
Old-fashioned lunch pail
On the table in the
Teachers' room, he

Announced his name and
Said technology education.
I added my name and German.
Both middle school teachers.

Telling him my love of
Wooden toys, he mentioned
The German toy factory
In a nearby town.

We called our project
The German Toyshop. I
Taught them German
He taught them how

To craft wooden toys.
Presented at conferences.
They learned two languages
Simultaneously.

During my teaching career, I have had some notable experiences. One such was teaching with Old Dominion University on the Navy Base in Norfolk, Virginia. I wore security identification dog tags to the class of about fifteen Navy SEAL officers and UDTs. Surrounded in mystery, these men could tell no one about their work, not even their families.

High Security Area

Teaching German to the
Officers of the Navy SEALS as
Well as the UDTs was
Interesting. Dog

Tag identification around
My neck, I entered
The building and
Was escorted to my

Classroom as well
As to the water
Fountain. No
Wandering around

Unchaperoned. This
Class fascinated me
Like no other. Very serious
But enthusiastic to learn.

Our friendship with Stan and Anna and their family began in Upstate New York where we lived near one another. Our daughter brought Anna some fresh parsley from our garden and returned grinning from ear to ear with a plate of homemade cookies Anna had just baked. Thus began years of friendship and many stories about escaping communist Czechoslovakia.

Fresh Parsley

Fresh parsley from
The garden and
Carried by my
Four year old

To the neighbor
Across the street.
Until now we had
Only waved

Beaming from
Ear to ear
Our daughter returned
With home baked cookies.

An instant friendship
Forged, we exchanged
Stories with
Our new friends.

Our dear friends Stan and Anna live near us in Upstate New York. They escaped from the former communist Czechoslovakia along with their two children. The next poems recount their escape.

Incredible Journey

She told me her
Story by the lake
As we walked that
Winter morning.

Snow and wind
Whipped at our faces.
She told me her
Incredible journey

Of coming to America
After escaping.
This modern day odyssey
Brought them to us.

Freedom smelled so
Sweet to them after
Hardships and grief.
The human spirit prevailed.

After the October Revolution the kulaks opposed collectivization of land, but in 1929 Stalin initiated their liquidation. Tough times ensued.

The Kulak

Landowner and
Farmer until
The Communists
Oppressed.

Opposed to
Collectivization of
Land, he refused
To bend.

Jailed for over
Three years
His uncle did
Not change his mind.

This would be
Something to tell
Grandchildren
Someday.

This poem tells a sad story about living conditions in communist Czechoslovakia. Stan told me they never broke his father's spirit nor any of his relatives.

In a Town called Jachymov

Sentenced to eight
Years prison, his father
Dug for uranium ore
For Soviet nuclear bombs.

He didn't know
That he would
Later die of
Lung cancer

At age sixty-two
From exposure to
Radioactivity in the
Town called Jachymov.

This was his price
To pay for refusing
The Communists.
They never broke him.

ABOUT THE AUTHOR

Born in Massachusetts and reared in Colorado, Mary Ann Niemczura has lived in Upstate New York for thirty years. She holds a Ph.D. degree, has lived and studied extensively in Germany including as a Fulbright Exchange Teacher twice, and currently teaches German at the high school level.

This poetical memoir recalls fond childhood memories in Massachusetts as seen through the author's eyes and those of her sisters. These are followed by life in Colorado, Germany and Central New York. It is intended to document those memories for future generations and for anyone interested in such tales.

Childhood in rural Western Massachusetts in the 1940s and early 1950s offered carefree days filled with playing, learning and exploring with minimal adult supervision. The poems may evoke fond memories of one's own youth.

CPSIA information can be obtained at www.ICGtesting.com
Printed in the USA
BVOW04s0929020714

357935BV00003B/9/P